WALKING CL(

GW00384400

the MALVERN

Number Sixty Nine in the popular series of walking guides

Contents

The hills themselves are criss-crossed with well used paths and it is difficult to get lost for long, so park up and explore!

Walked, Written and Drawn by Clive Brown
© Clive Brown 2012 - 14

Published by Clive Brown
ISBN 978-1-907669-69-9

PLEASE
Take care of the countryside
Your leisure is someone's livelihood

Close gates
Start no fires
Keep away from livestock and animals
Do not stray from marked paths
Take litter home
Do not damage walls, hedgerows or fences
Cross only at stiles or gates
Protect plants, trees and wildlife
Keep dogs on leads
Respect crops, machinery and rural property
Do not contaminate water

Although not essential we recommend good walking boots; during hot weather take something to drink on the way. All walks can easily be negotiated by an averagely fit person. The routes have been recently walked and surveyed, changes can however occur, please follow any signed diversions. Some paths cross fields which are under cultivation. All distances and times are approximate.

The maps give an accurate portrayal of the area, but scale has however been sacrificed in some cases for the sake of clarity and to fit restrictions of page size.

Walking Close To have taken every care in the research and production of this guide but cannot be held responsible for the safety of anyone using them.

During very wet weather, parts of these walks may become impassable through flooding, check before starting out. Stiles and rights of way can get overgrown during the summer; folding secateurs are a useful addition to a walker's rucksack.

Thanks to Angela for help in production of these booklets

Views or comments?
walkingcloseto@yahoo.co.uk

69:A

Walking Close to the Malvern Hills

Malvern is simply translated from the Old English a 'Bare Hill'. The line of pointy mountains running south from Worcester, on the western side of the M5, give the impression from the motorway of great height; in truth they are only of medium height compared to most English and Welsh mountains. Extending north-south for nine miles and never wider than a mile at the widest close to Great Malvern. The altitude is exaggerated by the steep sides of the hills and the low land of the Severn Valley. The highest point at Worcestershire Beacon is 1394ft, the smaller hills close by the beacon range from 1100ft to 1300ft. The southern, lower part of the hills are dominated by the British Camp Iron Age fort, on the Herefordshire Beacon, which is 1109ft. The hills are the most striking part of a geological fault line running north-south parallel to the Welsh border. The igneous content of these hills has proved to be harder wearing than the surrounding countryside.

The town and its various suburbs are built partly on the slope at the side of the Hills although the A449 road passing through between Worcester and Ledbury keeps to a fairly level course. The prevalent Italianate architecture of large houses and disused hotels now converted to apartments, provides the newcomer with instant Swiss style vistas. The town grew around the priory first established here at the end of the 11th century. At the reformation in 1541 the town bought the priory church for £20 to replace their own less illustrious building.

Malvern Water has been popular for over 400 years and is partly the story of three Queens. Elizabeth I was the first monarch to be seen drinking the water publicly, Queen Victoria is said never to have travelled without it and our present Queen is reputed to take it with her all over the world. The water is still bottled on a small scale by a local company, but the main factory which had been bottling water since the mid 19th century was closed down as unprofitable by Coca Cola/Schweppes in 2010.

The Downs Light Railway (walk no 3) is thought to be the world's oldest private miniature railway. It was built in 1925 by Geoffrey Hoyland, headmaster of the adjacent Downs School and used for educational purposes. After the departure of Hoyland the railway was allowed to descend into dereliction until it was rescued during the 1970s by James Boyd and former pupils. The railway steams occasionally for school and charity events.

We feel that it would be difficult to get lost with the instructions and map in this booklet, but recommend carrying an Ordnance Survey map. Walk no 9 appears on Explorer Map No 204, the rest of the walks are on the Explorer Malverns area map no 190; Landranger no 150 covers at a smaller scale. Roads, geographical features and buildings, not on our map but visible from the walk can be easily identified.

1   Madresfield Court

6¹/₂ Miles   3¹/₄ Hours

Use the car park at Old Hills on the B4224 south of Callow End. No facilities.

1   Leave the car park out of the car entrance and walk along the grass verge towards Callow End, as the road swings left, keep straight on along the road downhill towards Pixham Ferry.

2   At the junction, take the tarmac farm driveway to the right; keep straight on as the track bears right up to Pixham Farm, through the gates and on to the hardcore farm road. Follow the road to the gate at the field entrance, go through, cross the field and go through the next gate to the top of the embankment.

3   Continue through the metal gate and across the footbridge; follow the track uphill with the hedge left. At an unmarked point bear right, along the track with the hedge to the right, passing right of Clevelode village and down the stony drive to the road. Carry on to the crossroads at the B4224.

4   Turn right, along the grass verge of this busy road and bear left into the lay-by. Go into the driveway of Whiteacres Farm, through the gate on the right and up the path between the fence and the dyke. Step over the stile and continue with the fence to the left, across the next stile; turn right, into the corner and left to the marker post. Take the field edge right with the hedge to the right. At an unmarked point bear left across the field which may be under cultivation although a path should be well marked within any crop, to the hedge gap at the corner ahead. Go through and maintain direction to the gate at the hedge ahead.

5   Take the farm road to the left, with the fence to the left; all the way to Home Farm. Continue between the farm buildings and follow the drive out and over the cattle grid to the road. Turn right, along the grass verge of this busy road, through Madresfield village and past the church.

6   As the road swings left, turn right along the signposted driveway; bear right at the junction and carry on through the sunken road and under the bridges to a metal kissing gate next to a wide wooden gate. Go through and bear left to the hedge, follow this field edge left/straight on for nearly a mile, through two boundaries to a footbridge at Madresfield Brook.

7   Cross and bear slight right across the field and over the stony farm road; go up the field edge with New Coppice to the left and through the kissing gate. Turn right, along the track to the alternative parking area; cross the grass to the left, up the slope and into the trees. Go between the concrete posts back into the Old Hills parking area to find your vehicle.

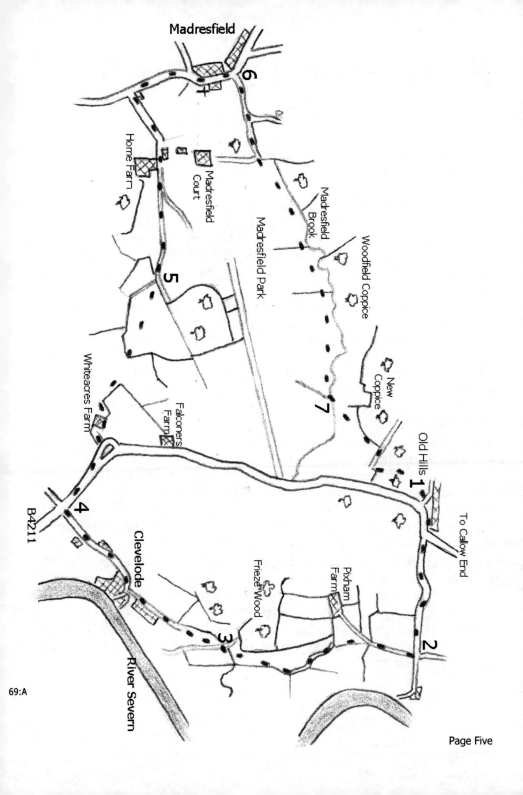

Madresfield

Madresfield Court

Home Farm

Madresfield Park

Madresfield Brook

Woodfield Coppice

New Coppice

Whiteacres Farm

Falconers Farm

Old Hills

To Callow End

B4211

Clevelode

Frieze Wood

Pixham Farm

River Severn

1
2
3
4
5
6
7

69:A

2   Blackmore Wood

4³/₄ Miles   2¹/₄ Hours

Find a parking space in Hanley Swan; no toilets. Post Office/shop, pub the 'Swan' and local butchers shop. Start from the crossroads.

1   Go down Welland Road, towards Gloucester, past the school and village hall and take the bridleway to the right. Continue to the end and go through the gate close to the wooden chalet. Walk up the left hand field edge into the left hand corner and cross the tarmac driveway at Merebrook Farm. Bear right from the gate, over the field to the right hand gate, carry on ahead up the wide track between the fence and the hedge to the stile on the left.

2   Bear right, across a stile and keep ahead on the tarmac road between fences, passing right of the factory unit. Bear right to the stile on the right, step over and follow the fence ahead, then left over a stile to the road. Turn right for 40yds and cross this busy road carefully.

3   Take the footpath ahead between the bungalow and the house; keep direction past the farm buildings and all the way through Blackmore Wood. Exit over the footbridge/stile and bear left across the stile in the far left corner, turn left along the field edge with the trees to the left, through the gate and the trees.

4   Cross the driveway and keep ahead up the narrow path between fences, over a stile and the next field. Go through the metal gates left of the farm buildings and bear right, over stiles either side of a farm road. Cross this field to the stile left of the white house and carry on to the bridleway signpost.

5   Turn right, along Hawthorn Lane, upslope to the signpost, step over the stile and follow the field edge right. Turn left at the end along the wide track and keep ahead through gates to the signpost on the right.

6   Go over and turn left back to the original direction with the hedge now left, cross the stile at the far end of this long field and continue upslope over the next stile. Continue up the track between trees to a crossroads of paths.

7   Turn right, over the stile and cross the field and the stile ahead. Keep ahead downhill, between the blocks of trees and carry on right of Stable Farm, along the tarmac road and over the bridge. Keep on this road all the way back to Hanley Swan to find your vehicle.

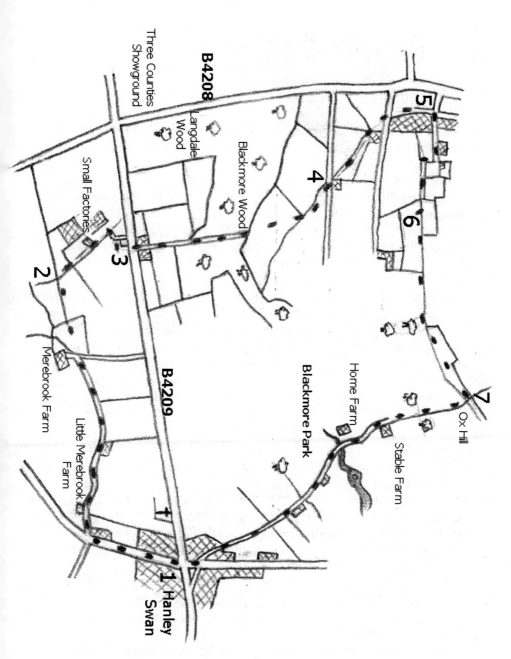

3   Brockhill Lane

$6^3/_4$ Miles $3^1/_4$ Hours

Find a parking space in Colwall Stone on the B4218 south west of Malvern, no toilets but all other facilities in the village.

1   Start from the crossroads at the centre of the village close by the 'Colwall Park Hotel'. Go down Stone Drive to the signpost at the Stone Drive sign, take the narrow signposted path and carry on up the tarmac path between houses. Cross the road and keep straight on over a busier road, past a byway signpost and continue upslope between trees. Keep direction from the gate on the right, between the hedge and the fence, past the tennis courts to the signpost on the private road.

2   Take the wide hardcore road left/ahead and carry on upslope *(watch out for the miniature railway tunnel)*. Just beyond the crossroads of tracks at the lime kilns, step over the stile on the left and continue the original direction with the trees and road now right. Carry on left/straight on to two stiles close to a row of houses.

3   Keep straight on up the hardcore/tarmac roadway to the road and turn right for 60yds to the signpost for Mathon. Turn left along the tarmac driveway and at the marker post bear left, still on the road. Cross the stile and fork right, with the hedge to the right, to the stile in the corner. Keep straight on along the wider track, through trees, downslope and cross the tarmac road.

4   Follow the narrow road ahead as it turns left downslope and back up, past some houses to a marker disc at the gate in front of Bank Farm. Bear left to a marked, wide metal gate.

5   Keep ahead downslope through the field and the gate. Bear left through this next field and follow the track through two gates; continue ahead on the path along the edge of the trees, through the gate at the end. Carry on with the trees now right, through the kissing gate and into the gravel yard at Rose Farm; bear left down to the road.

6   Turn right, up to the junction and take the road left for 120yds to the signpost. Turn left, through the hedge gap and walk round the cricket pitch; go through the gap left of the pavilion. Bear right, through the gate and keep ahead through the trees to the road at Moat Farm.

7   Take the road right, to the junction and bear left, signposted South Hyde, to the signpost on the left. Turn left along the left hand field edge to the stile at the end, step over and turn right. Continue on the original direction with the hedge now right, bearing left to the footbridge.

Bank Farm 5

Park Farm 4

Rose Farm 6
Lane End
Mathon Court
Mathon Lodge
3

Moat Farm 7

8

Brockhill Road

Tunnel
Miniature Railway 2

9

10

1 Station
Colwall Stone

Page Nine

B4218

Completed on the next Page (Ten)

8   Cross and keep ahead with the hedge to the left, over the stile in the corner and continue direction over the footbridge in the far corner. Carry on along the field edge to the corner and walk across the field ahead. This field may be under cultivation although a track should be well marked within any crop. Continue across a stile and the next field with the trees now left, past a metal gate and go over the stile/footbridge at the bottom. Bear left over the stile left of the trees.

9   Keep straight on, with the trees to the right, over the next stile and follow the path ahead, through trees and cross the footbridge/stile. Bear left on the path with the fence to the right, walk across the concrete parking area and bear left between hedges. Take the wide gravel path between hedges to the road.

10 Turn right for 110yds to the signpost and take the wide gravel track; keep direction through kissing gate, over a footbridge and the open field, bearing left, through the kissing gate to the road. Turn right, to the main B4218 at the junction and take the roadside path left, back to the village centre and your vehicle.

---

4   Gullet Quarry

$4^1/_2$ Miles $2^1/_4$ Hours

Use the British Camp car park on the A449 south of Malvern, pay and display; café and toilets close by.

1   Cross the road and go down the road ahead to the signpost, fork left downslope away from the toilets , past the brick tank and over the stile. Follow the path through the trees to the junction just past the signpost, turn sharp left, back upslope and bear right on the narrow track past the marker post. Step over the stile and carry on upslope; bear right on the wider track to the road.

2   Turn left along the grass verge to the signpost and cross this busy road carefully. Take the wide stony track upslope, past a stile close to a round topped concrete reservoir and bear right at a marker post at a fork. Continue for nearly a mile to a wide metal gate close to a cattle grid with high metal fences.

3   Turn left on a tarmac path, downslope between hedges, signposted Gullet Quarry. As this path turns right, bear left on a steep track downhill to the road; continue on the road back up to the car park.

4   At the green barrier on the left opposite the car park entrance take the obvious path curving left through the grass, all the way to a signpost. Keep direction upslope on the stony driveway.

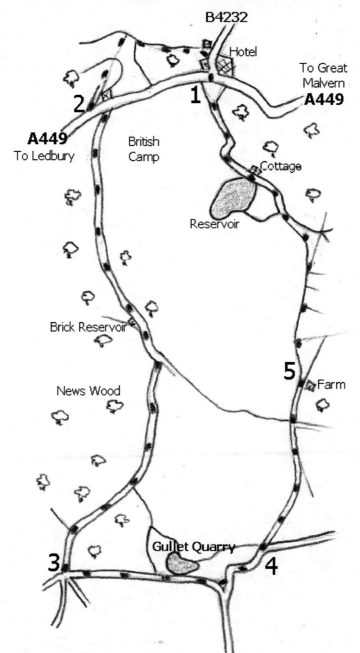

B4232

Hotel

To Great
Malvern
A449

1

2

A449
To Ledbury

British
Camp

Cottage

Reservoir

Brick Reservoir

News Wood

69:A

5

Farm

3

Gullet Quarry

4

5 Just past a farm as the track opens out, bear left on the grassy track closer to the trees on the left. Continue with the sharper slope up to the left, bearing left through the edge of the trees. Follow the steep concrete track past the reservoir and the tarmac drive through the trees, leading past the gate into the car park to find your vehicle.

...path through the field, step over the stile and continue left/straight on, between trees. Go through a kissing gate and keep ahead, still between trees. Bear left through the next kissing gate and carry on still downhill, with the trees to the right, to the metal gate at the bottom; bear right, to the road.

3 Turn left to the signpost at the gateway and turn right, up the gravel driveway right of the house at Rose Farm, through the wide gate on the right and the kissing gate. Follow the track ahead past the marker post and through the gate at the top left. Bear left on the path through the edge of the trees and exit through the gate. Keep direction through the next gate and carry on up the narrow field bearing right to a gate, go through and continue upslope through the gate and the wide marked gate ahead at the top.

4 Turn left and right, between the houses at Bank Farm; keep ahead over a stile and bear right, downslope with the trees to the right. Cross the stile, keep direction through trees and bear left to a stile; step over and bear right over a stile close by on the right. Bear left between the trees and the fence to a marker post.

5 Take the track sharp right, upslope, to the top of the ridge; turn right and almost immediate left, down the steep slope the opposite side. Carry on with the trees right, through the halfway gate, down over the stream and through the gate at the bottom. Bear left uphill, over the left hand stile and bear slight right, uphill to the unseen stile at the top, left of the low green building.

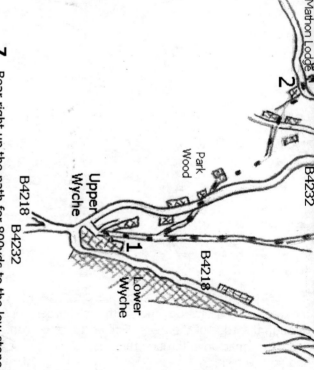

Mathon Lodge

B4232

Park Wood

Upper Wyche

B4218

B4232

B4218

Lower Wyche

7 Bear right up the path for 800yds to the low stone direction cairn, turn left towards Great Malvern and immediate right up the path with Table Hill to the left, bearing left into the dip at the top with the path left of the Sugarloaf Hill summit; continue over the angled crossroads, up the path to the toposcope and Ordnance Survey post at the top of Worcestershire Beacon.

8 Take the main path south, which leads eventually to the car park at beacon Road and your vehicle.

Worcestershire Beacon

Use the Beacon Road pay and display car park at Upper Wyche. Toilets and other facilities close by.

1 Walk further uphill to the fork with a wide track and bear left on the track downhill; cont nue further downhill on a narrower path to the B4232 road. Turn right for 200yds and bear left on a double hardcore track; as the track swings left through a gate at a bungalow, keep straight on up a narrower path, bearing left through trees to a narrow tarmac road. Cross and carry on, parallel to the telegraph poles to the road at Park Farm and turn left for 35yds to the signpost.

6 Follow the hardcore road to the left and continue as it winds through the Field Centre and the allotments to the road. Keep direction to the main road close to the 'Lamb'. Turn right, to the pub and left up Lamb Bank to the signpost at the top. Carry on up the narrow concrete path and go through the gate.

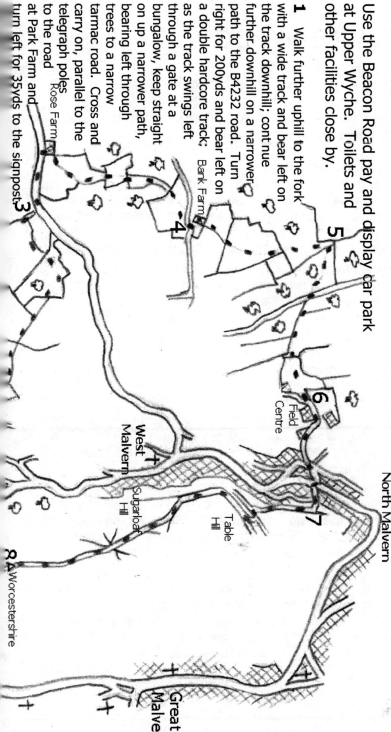

North Malvern

Bank Farm

Rose Farm

West
Malvern

Sugarloaf
Hill

Field
Centre

Table
Hill

Great
Malver

Worcestershire

6   Six Acre Wood

4³/₄ Miles   2¹/₄ Hours

Find a roadside parking space in West Malvern, no toilets. Local pubs the 'Lamb Inn' and the 'Brewers Arms'.

1 Go down Croft Bank and turn right into Croft Farm Drive. Continue through Croft Farm down the wide sunken track and go through a wide then a narrow gate; carry on to a marker post and take the farm track to the right, for 120yds to the next marker post on the left. Bear left; downslope again with the trees to the right; then further down, past a tall marker post to the corner of the trees. Continue down the sunken path in the trees, over the stile on to a narrow tarmac road.

2 Take this road right/straight on and follow it upslope, passing right of the house and left of Bank Farm. The track continues on a hardcore surface, through a gate and along the right hand slope of the valley to a gated junction.

3 Turn right, along the path between the fence and the trees; keep on this track bearing left through the trees and follow as it descends to a marker post on the right. Take the narrow path, still through trees, up the slight slope, then down over a stile. Keep ahead with the trees to the right, down past the fence corner to the gate on the right.

4 Turn right, through the gate and follow the field edge left, with the fence then the trees to the left, to the footbridge in the corner. Cross and turn left, along the path round the base of the hill to a marker post at a junction. Turn right, with the stream still right; keep on the track right of the first stile, still at the bottom of the slope. Bear right, slightly uphill close to the second stile. As the trees end, keep direction through the field and between the farm buildings; bear left to the road.

4 Turn right and follow the road right, to a T-junction. Turn right and bear left, still on the road for 420yds to the signpost on the left. Step over the stile and go up the wide hedged track, take the right hand track and continue upslope through the edge of the trees. Go past the top corner of the field to the marker post at the top of the ridge.

5 Follow the path to the right, through the trees to a stile, cross and carry on with the trees to the left over the next stile and keep ahead through trees again. The track continues direction with a field sloping away to the right and leads eventually through a farmyard to the wide sunken road at the beginning of the walk. Turn left, through Croft Farm back into West Malvern to find your vehicle.

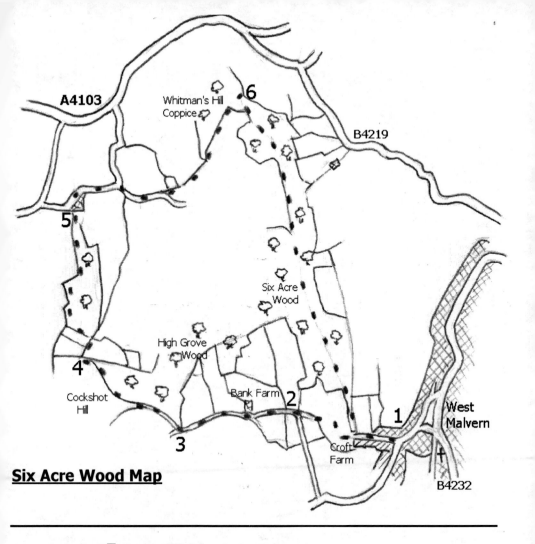

Six Acre Wood Map

Completion of 7 North Hill from Page Sixteen

3   Take the unmarked track up the stiff slope to the top of North Hill, over the summit and back down to Lady Howard de Walden Drive. Go along the path to the south (right/straight on) and follow the track to the top of Beacon Hill. Continue down the far side to the gravel path and a seat close to a litter cairn.

4   Turn back sharp left and bear right on a fairly level narrow path; bear right again keeping level and descend into a dip, go over a path and join a wider path left keeping more or less level again, around the hill to the corner of a zigzag. Continue right/straight on downslope and turn right, past a 'Beacon' cairn and left down the track to the upper extension of St Ann's Road.

5   Turn right, down into Great Malvern to find your vehicle.

North Hill

$3^1/_2$ Miles

2 Hours

Find a parking space in Great Malvern, all facilities in the town. Start from the Tourist Information Centre.

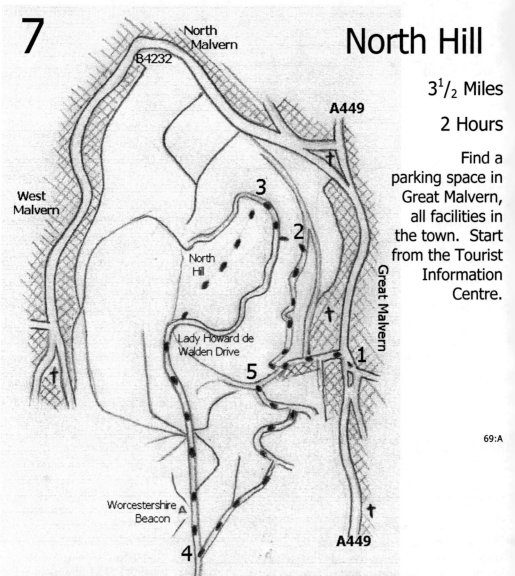

69:A

1 Go up to the T-junction on the main A449, turn right and immediate left into St Ann's Road. Follow the road uphill, keep ahead at the junction and up the slope to the 'No Turning' sign. Turn sharp right on the narrow path, with the slope of the hill up to the left and fork left further uphill.

2 At a fork marked by a stone cairn direction to North Hill bear left along the path and up the zigzag to the more substantial Lady Howard de Walden Drive. Turn right, along this path to the northernmost point of the left hand curve.

Instructions completed on the bottom of the previous Page (Fifteen).

8   British Camp

3 Miles   1³/₄ Hours

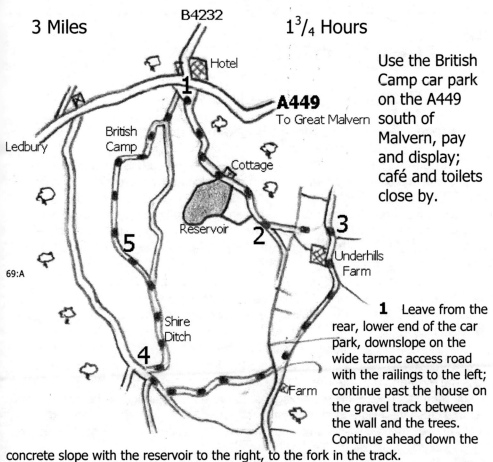

Use the British Camp car park on the A449 south of Malvern, pay and display; café and toilets close by.

1   Leave from the rear, lower end of the car park, downslope on the wide tarmac access road with the railings to the left; continue past the house on the gravel track between the wall and the trees. Continue ahead down the concrete slope with the reservoir to the right, to the fork in the track.

2   Take the lower, left hand, narrower path through the gate and bear left past the left of the tree, over the field and through the gate on to the concrete farm road.

3   Turn right, past Underhills Farm, through the gate and bear right, upslope with the fence and hedge to the right. Go through the gate and follow the track across heathland to a double telegraph pole. Bear right on the path upslope, carry on passing right of the next double telegraph pole, continue further upslope to where the path levels out at a staggered junction of paths.

4   Take the path right, up the stiffer slope to a T-junction with a path on a slight embankment above Shire Ditch; follow this path right to a simple flat top double seat. Bear left on a narrower path past a toposcope.

Instructions completed on the next Page (Eighteen)

5 Continue straight on up a stepped path and keep direction to the top of Herefordshire Beacon within the Iron Age fort known as British Camp. Take the steps and path down to a T-junction with a more substantial path and turn right, back to the car park and your vehicle.

9 Leigh Brook

6 Miles   3 Hours

Find a roadside parking space in Brockamin; no facilities.

1 Start from the junction of the main road and Dingle Road. Step over the stile opposite the end of Dingle Road and turn right, through the narrow gate. Cross the small field on a diagonal, through the gate and the gate at the other end of the barn. Continue through the gate in the dip and bear right, upslope through the metal gate in the hedge; keep ahead to the fence. Turn right, with the fence left and go over the fence in the corner. Turn left on the wide track downslope to the awkward stile on the right at Leigh Brook.

2 Scramble over and take the track through the rough area (it may be easier to use the bank at the edge of the field). Bear left across the stile and follow the edge of the brook over the next two stiles. Keep ahead across a field and step over the stile at the top right.

3 Bear left downslope, along the wide mud track and step over the stile. Keep ahead through the trees, with the brook to the left, up the slope and down again. Cross the dyke and the stile the other side, bear right parallel to the brook over the stile on the left. Take a left hand diagonal to the stile/footbridge in the hedge, step over and cross the field ahead which may be under cultivation although a path should be well marked within any crop. Go over the stile next to the metal gate and continue direction across the field to the road.

4 Turn left along the road up to the T-junction, turn left and immediate right, through the gate at the signpost. Keep ahead on the wide track between fields, into the dip and follow the narrower sunken path back upslope between hedges. The more substantial path continues direction back downslope between hedges to the road. Take the road left for 400yds to the signpost on the right (where the houses on the left start again).

5 Cross the stile and descend the steps into The Dingle, carry on over the wood and then the brick footbridge; take the path upslope through the edge of the trees. Keep straight on across the field ahead which may be under cultivation although a path should be well marked within any crop. Follow the farm road left and right, between the buildings and bear left along the tarmac driveway to the road.

6 Turn left for 175yds to the signpost on the right and turn right, past the white house and bear left, along the field edge with the hedge to the left. Continue along the field edge with the hedge to the left, through the right hand gap in the corner and carry on, hedge still left to the far corner of the trees.

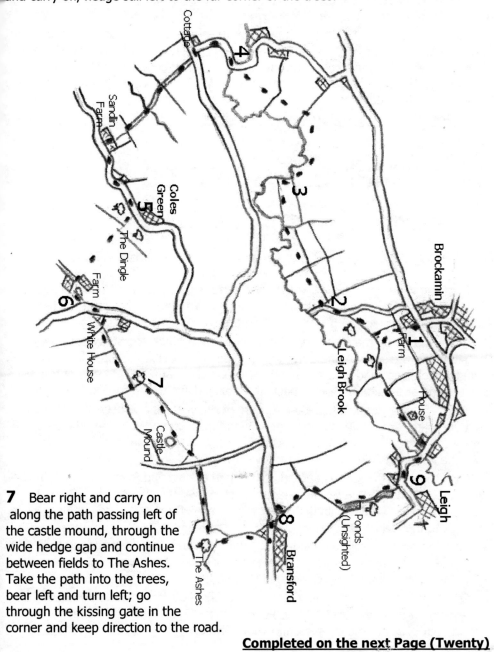

7 Bear right and carry on along the path passing left of the castle mound, through the wide hedge gap and continue between fields to The Ashes. Take the path into the trees, bear left and turn left; go through the kissing gate in the corner and keep direction to the road.

Completed on the next Page (Twenty)

8   Turn left for 160yds to the signpost and take the path to the right, follow the right hand field edge through the wide gap in the corner and turn right, over the stile in the boundary to the corner at the trees. Turn left along the field edge with the trees and the ponds to the right, down to the road in Leigh.

9   Take the road left, back over Leigh Brook to the footpath signpost; turn left down the driveway, across the paved area right of the house and over the stile at the back.   Bear right, upslope along the right hand field edge at the top of the slope and go through the gate. Continue on the left hand field edge and bear right, to the gate in the hedge passed through near the beginning of the walk; retrace steps downslope and right of the farm to Brockamin and your vehicle.

10   Malvern Common

$4^1/_4$ Miles $2^3/_4$ Hours

Use the car park off the B4218 at Lower Wyche, pay and display, no facilities.

1   Start from the Upper car park; take the narrow zigzag path upslope signposted to the Worcestershire Beacon. Join the tarmac path at the top near the Gold Mine Plinth and turn left (south) past the parking area, down to the road.

2   Cross and go up the steps opposite and bear left; follow the stony path uphill. Continue over the summit and down to a junction of paths in the dip. Bear left down through trees and follow the path in a semi-circle around the edge of the hill, to a junction at a hairpin. Double back and zigzag down to the road at Holywell.

3   Turn left, past Benbow Close and turn right down steps and between fences to the main road. Cross this junction carefully and keep straight on along the footpath ahead, downslope and over the access road. Carry on over the stile at the gate, down the left hand field edge and step over the stile.

4   Take the wide track left, bear left at the marker post and follow the track to the T-junction. Turn right, under the bridge and step over the stile on the left; keep direction parallel to the dismantled railway line bear left up steps and continue along the track to the road.

5   Turn left over the railway bridge; bear right, through the small parking area and across the scrubland to the track at the corner of a low stone wall. Take this wide stony track right, all the way to the road (the A449).

6   Cross carefully, go through the gap right of the '40' sign and take the path through the trees, over Lower Wyche Road to the B4218. Turn left, along the roadside path back to the car park and your vehicle.

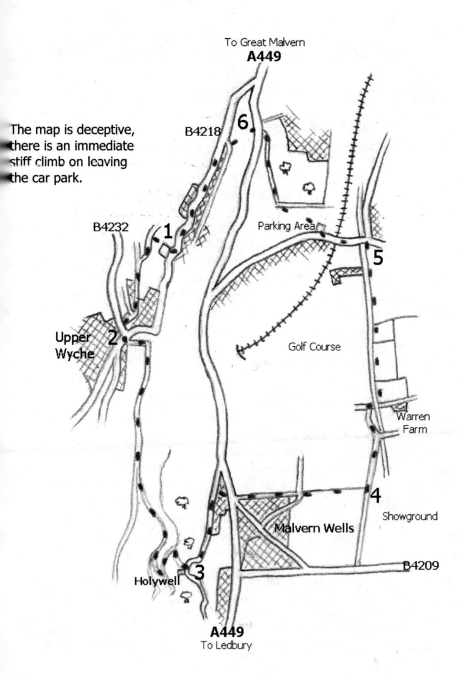

The map is deceptive, there is an immediate stiff climb on leaving the car park.

To Great Malvern
A449

B4218

6

B4232

1

Parking Area

5

Upper
Wyche

2

Golf Course

Warren
Farm

4

Showground

Malvern Wells

B4209

Holywell

3

A449
To Ledbury

69:A

11 Croome Landscape Park

$3^1/_2$ Miles $1^3/_4$ Hours

Find a parking space in High Green. NT members will probably find it easier to use the parking space at Croome and start at the church.

1   Walk down to the east end of the village and go through the hedge gap on the right by the double signpost. Cross the field ahead, just slightly to the right, to the marker disc on the post left of the pond; the field may be under cultivation but a path should be well marked within any crop. Continue through the gap along the field edge with the fence and the trees to the right, through the kissing gate in the next corner. Keep ahead on the right hand field edge with the fence and the hedge to the right, up the short slope to the top right corner.

2   Bear right to the kissing gate near the church. Go through the gate left of the church, through the churchyard and keep ahead to the road. Turn right, along the grass verge to the stile on the right, just around the left hand corner.

3   Step over and keep direction along the narrow concrete farm road and the field for two thirds of a mile to the stile by the gate at the trees. Go through the trees and exit through the gate the other side.

4   Take the field edge to the right, with the trees to the right, over the stile in the corner and down the slope. Cross the next stile and continue past the sluice and the marker post to a wooden gate.

5   Go through and take a right hand diagonal away from the Croome River to the kissing gate right of Westfield Farm. Continue up the farm road between trees and through the gate, carry on along the road to the right, with the park to the right.

6   As the road swings left, cross the footbridge/stile ahead and bear left across the field which may be under cultivation to the narrow hedge gap near High Green used at the start of the walk. Turn left back to the village to find your vehicle.

The Croome Court estate was formerly the country seat of the Earls of Coventry. In 1751, the 6th Earl employed Lancelot 'Capability' Brown (1716-1783) with his first major architectural work. Some of the interior of the house is attributed to the architect Robert Adam. Brown landscaped the parkland to include a wide river and lake system and a number of classical temples and follies which he called 'eyecatchers'.

69:A

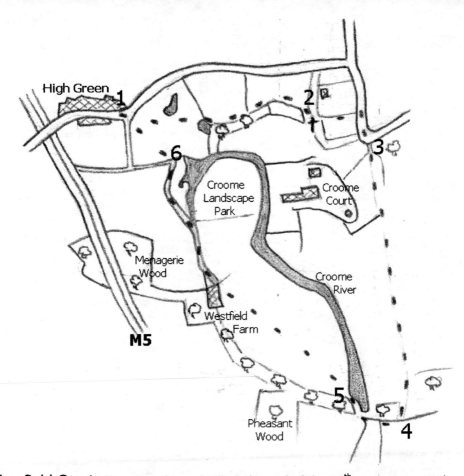

Madresfield Court, (Page Four) was built at the end of the 16th century, around the existing Great Hall built at the end of the 12th century. It was again rebuilt at the end of the Victorian era with a look to reinforce its Tudor origins. The property has always belonged to the Lygon family who were Earls of Beauchamp until the death of the 8th Earl in 1979. It is now looked after by the Elmley Foundation. Madresfield Court and the Lygon Family are believed to have been the inspiration for the Flyte Family and 'Brideshead Revisited' by Evelyn Waugh. The television version was filmed in Castle Howard and faraway Yorkshire. Plans were made just before World War II for the government to relocate to Worcester in the event of an invasion; Madresfield would have been used to house the royal family.

Jenny Lind (1820-87), affectionately known as the 'Swedish Nightingale' achieved fame as an international opera star. She toured extensively in Europe, Great Britain and America. From 1855 she lived in England, giving concerts and teaching. She retired to Wynd's Point near British Camp in the Malverns and is buried in Great Malvern.

The 'Walking Close to' Series

South and South West

The New Forest (North and West)
Romsey and the Test Valley
Cheddar Gorge
Exmouth and East Devon
Corsham and Box (Wiltshire)
The Quantock Hills (West Somerset)
Blandford Forum (Dorset)

The New Forest (South and East)
The East Devon Coast
Glastonbury and the City of Wells
The Avon near Bath
The Avon near Chippenham (Wiltshire)
Shaftesbury (Dorset)
Bradford-on-Avon (Wiltshire)

East Anglia and Lincolnshire

The Nene near Peterborough
Lavenham (Suffolk)
The Nene Valley Railway near Wansford
The Nene near Oundle
The Great North Road near Stilton
Bury St Edmunds
Norfolk Broads (Northern Area)
Southwold and the Suffolk Coast
North West Norfolk (Hunstanton and Wells)
North Norfolk (Cromer and Sheringham)
The Lincolnshire Wolds (North)
The Stour near Sudbury (Suffolk)
Chelmsford
Epping Forest (Essex/North London)
The Colne near Colchester
Thetford Forest (Norfolk/Suffolk)
The Great Ouse in Huntingdonshire
The Torpel Way (Stamford to Peterborough)

Grafham Water (Huntingdonshire)
Dedham Vale (Suffolk/Essex)
The Cam and the Granta near Cambridge
Lincoln
The Welland near Stamford
The Isle of Ely
Norfolk Broads (Southern Area)
Aldeburgh, Snape and Thorpeness
Clare, Cavendish and Haverhill
Bourne and the Deepings
The Lincolnshire Wolds (South)
The Orwell near Ipswich
Stowmarket (Suffolk)
Hertford and the Lee Valley
Newmarket
The Great Ouse near King's Lynn
South Lincolnshire

Midlands

The Nene near Thrapston
The Nene near Wellingborough
The River Ise near Kettering
The Nene near Northampton
Rockingham Forest (Northamptonshire)
Daventry and North West Northamptonshire
Rugby
Stratford-upon-Avon
Rutland Water
Eye Brook near Uppingham
The Soar near Leicester
Lutterworth (Leicestershire)
The Vale of Belvoir (North Leicestershire)
Melton Mowbray
The Welland near Market Harborough
Banbury
South West Herefordshire

The Great Ouse near Bedford
Woburn Abbey (Bedfordshire)
Sherwood Forest
Pitsford Water (Northamptonshire)
The Thames near Oxford
The Trent near Nottingham
The Vale of White Horse
Henley-on-Thames
The River Pang (Reading/Newbury)
The Great Ouse north of Milton Keynes
The Cotswolds near Witney
The Malvern Hills
The Dukeries (Sherwood Forest)
The Severn near Worcester
Woodstock and Blenheim Palace
The Kennet near Newbury

Cumbria

Cartmel and Southern Lakeland